# Food for Your M

## (God Help Us A

Lonnie C. Edwards Jr

**PUBLISHING INC.**
LONNIE C EDWARDS Jr.


EMAIL bigman2big7000@yahoo.com

**EDITED BY**
D.NOBLE
L.SISCO


**COVER AND ILLUSTRATION BY**
KRISTA MAESSER


**WRITTEN BY LONNIE C. EDWARDS**

THIS BOOK IS DEDICATED TO MY
MOTHER; MY FATHER; MY COUSIN, MARVIN WHITE
Jr.; AND TO EVERONE THAT HAS A PROBLEM,
NEEDS A FRIEND, OR HAS A HARD TIME
EXPRESSING HOW THEY FEEL. I AM HERE
TO TELL YOU GOD WILL PULL YOU
THROUGH IF YOU CAN STAND THE PULL.

It was not easy growing up in Illinois, especially when awaking to the sound of your mother and father fighting. Not knowing rather to pray, cry or shoot someone. It was confusing to see my father hurt my mother, not because he hated her but because he was stressed out and hurt himself. No, I did not like it, but what could I do? I was young, hurt, and confused myself. I loved my father. Every time they fought I felt God was with us, but I did not know why He put us allowed us to go through this drama. Maybe so we might become something, whether it is good or bad. I thank God for the drama, the slaps, beating and the hurt I experienced. I was young black and surrounded by dope, guns, and corrupt cops. What could I have done? I did not want to end up in jail, dead, or lost. So what could I do? I could have prayed; I knew how to pray. My mother and father were strong believers in God and lived it in spite of the trials and tribulations that occurred in our home. For a young man like me, life was hard. In case you haven't noticed, I have gone through my past quickly to make a point.

Life has been like a dream to me; like a dream, when you awake you're not sure if what you dreamed about was real or not. For example, a person spends all their life thinking how it would be when they get married, and the rest of the their life wondering how to get out of that same marriage. Marriage is beautiful when you find the right person. And if you believe that, you also believe that Peter Pan is a real little boy. It is my belief that there is no such thing as the right one, and as soon as people realize that life will be happier.

People have to grow in life, go through things in life, and rearrange things in life, in order for them to become "right" for each other in life. Marriage is fun, but you have to trust (or learn how to trust) or you will never accomplish anything together in life-from sports, education, love, and even taking care of problems. That is why I love to write. I am not a rocket scientist, but the words I feel are true and no one can take that from me. So I pray your souls are touched from my life experiences, poems, and feelings God has blessed me with.

# Table of Contents

## Section 4          Strength too all

Answer me                           Illustrations
Ladies
Brothers
Tired                               Illustrations
Clarity
Unsuccessful Thief
(Voices in my head)

## Section 5          God is a protector

Covered                             Illustrations
Peace of mind
Silent Night
Death through the wind
Running out time                    Illustrations
Bottom Line

## Section 6          Mental thought

*THEY*
*THOUGHTS*

# Section 1

Encouraging and Inspirations

# I CRIED

BOO HOO, LITTLE COUSIN, I SHEDDED THEM
PRAYING TO GOD, I COULD HAVE STOPPED HIM
FROM MAKING THE BIGGEST MISTAKE OF HIS LIFE
I WANTED TO FIGHT, SHOOT, CUT OFF HIS NUBBS, AND SHOW
HIM I WAS A TRUE THUG
BUT I KNEW THAT WASN'T GODS LOVE.
GOD FORGIVE ME FOR MY EVIL THOUGHTS
COUSIN FORGIVE ME FOR MY LOVE
UNABLE TO AVENGE YOUR DEATH IS A BURDEN ON MY SOUL.
I PRAY GOD WILL HELP ME MAINTAIN MY CONTROL.

In Loving Memory of
Marvin White, Jr.
1975 – 2001

# BROKEN YOKES

SISTER WHY DO YOU HATE HER SO MUCH,
SHE'S ONLY TRYING TO HELP YOU BECOME A WOMAN OF GOD
CRY NO MORE LITTLE ONE,
FOR I'M HERE TO BRING BREATH TO YOUR SOUL
I KNOW YOUR PAIN DAUGHTER, I KNOW YOUR FEARS,
KNOW I'M GOD, SO GIVE ME CHEERS
DWELL NOT ON THE PAST,
FOR IT WILL DESTROY YOUR BLESSING
DEFLATE YOUR GIFTS
AND IMPAIL YOUR HEART NOT TO FORGIVE
SEEK ME FOR GUIDANCE, NOT REVENGE
BELIEVE IN ME,
TRUST IN ME,
HAVE LOVE FOR ME
I WILL PROVIDE FOR YOU, I WILL FIGHT FOR YOU,
KNOW I'M GOD

## GET YOURS

MY MIND IS THIRSTY FOR KNOWLEDGE.
THE NEED FOR INTELLIGENCE GROWS MORE.
I CAN'T EXPLAIN IT, THE HUNGER IS SO DEEP
IT SEEPS THROUGH MY PORES.
TRAPPED AT SEA WITH A BOAT AND NO OARS,
NO ONE TO FEED ME, OR OPEN ANY DOORS
IN THIS WORLD, I HAVE TO TAKE MINE
WAITING FOR SOMEONE ELSE I'LL GO BLIND,
NOT BLIND TO THE FACT THAT I CAN'T SEE,
BUT BLIND TO THE FACT THAT I CAN'T BE SOMETHING I
WANT TO BE.
I STRIVE FOR MINE, CONTENT AS A DOVE, THANKING
GOD ALMIGHTY I DIDN'T SALE DRUGS.
I'M ABSORBING SO MUCH KNOWLEDGE,
IT WILL SEND YOU IN A PANIC.
FEEDING MY BRAIN WITH PLENTY OF
WISDOM, KNOWLEDGE, AND UNDERSTANDING
I'M SPEAKING ABOUT MAINTAINING.

# THE STRUGGLE

I'M BLEEDING INSIDE,
FROM THE ABSENT MINDLESS SPIRITUAL DEMONS
THAT
CARESSES AND POSSESSES MY PEOPLE.
CAUSING MISCHIEF AND MADNESS ON THIS HARSH AND CRUEL
PLANET
STANDING ON MY FEET FIRMLY WITH MY BACK AGAINST THE
WALL
KILLING EVERY DEMON THAT TRYS TO BOUNCE MY FAMILY LIKE
A BALL
PRAYING OFF EVILNESS,
SHOOTING SCRIPTURES LIKE A MAGNUM,
OUT NUMBERED, BUT EVERY SPIRIT I HIT GETS A BACK SPASM.
THE ENEMY HAS BEEN STICKING US WITH TRICKERY FOR
CENTURIES.
IT'S TIME FOR SAINTS TO START DAMAGING SATANS PLANS,
LEAVING HIM SOMETHING HE CAN'T COPE WITH, SO HE IS AS
HOPELESS AS A PENNY WITH A FOLD IN IT.
THE CUTS ARE HEALED,
AND THE BATTLE HAS BEEN CONSEALED,
SO SATAN JUST CHILL

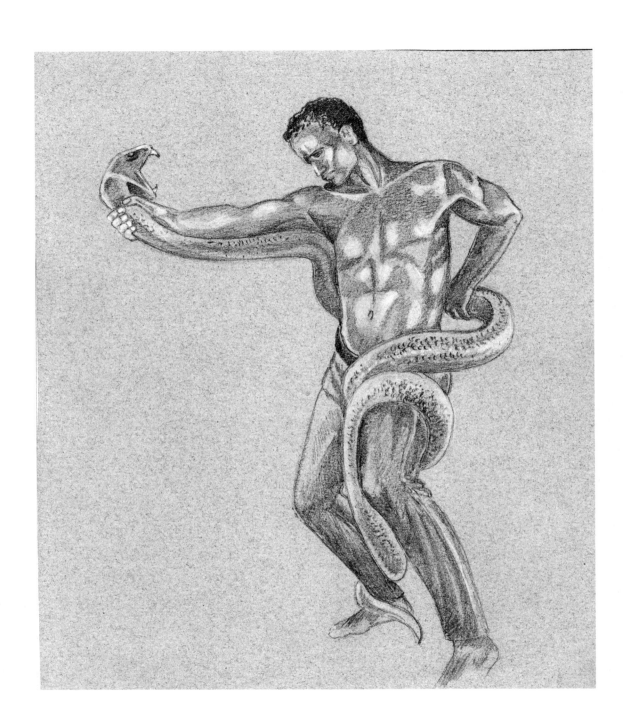

# WHERE DO WE GO FROM HERE

WHERE DO WE GO FROM HERE?
I ASKED MYSELF
WHERE DO WE GO?
AS THE CHILDREN PLAY IN THE PARK,
AND THE DOGS BARK IN THE DARK.
POVERTY DEPRESSES,
SATAN PROGRESSES IN INFECTING,
AND POSSESING OUR PEOPLE OF TODAY
AND CHILDREN OF TOMORROW
HE BRINGS SORROW AND TEARS,
THAT PIERCES THE HEARTS OF FAMILIES
WHO LIVE IN PAIN AND AGONY?
SO WHAT DO WE DO TO KEEP OUR SPIRITS FREE, SOUL BLESSED,
CLEAN AND REFRESHED?
SO WE CAN EXCEL FROM HELL AND GO WHERE ANGELS DWELL.
THAT WE MAY SMELL SWEET VICTORY AND MAKE HISTORY
WHEN WE OPEN OUR EYES,
WE WILL SEE WITHOUT FEAR,
WE DO KNOW WHERE WE GO FROM HERE,
TO HEAVEN

# MOMMA DON'T CRY

BLEEDING INSIDE OVER THE PAST TRAGEDIES
UNPURE SCENES CLOUD HER LIFESPAN,
MOMMA WHY ARE YOU CRYING?
PAIN DILUTES HER SOUL
MASSIVE UNBALANCED FEELINGS
BREAKS DOWN HER CONTROL
MOMMA WHY ARE YOU CRYING?
MENTAL, PHYSICAL, AND EMOTIONAL ABUSE
SATURATES HER SPIRIT
SO ONLY A WHISPER CAN HEAR IT.
THE UNTAME PAST
HAS MADE THE FUTURE HARD TO LIVE IN
SHE'S UNABLE TO GROW,
THE HOLD THAT THE PAST HAS
IS REFUSING TO LET HER GO,
MOMMA WHY ARE YOU CRYING?
FATHER DIDN'T MEAN IT,
HE ALLOWED THE DEVIL TO GET IN IT.
HE DIDN'T KNOW LOVE WAS ABOVE HIM,
HE DIDN'T LET HIS TROUBLES LEAVE HIM.
HE DIDN'T LET GOD LEAD HIM,
BUT HE LOVED US ALL
AND BEHIND EVERY PAINFUL FALL,
THERE'S A GREAT WATERFALL.

# TRAPPED

SOCIETY HAS ME TRAPPED.
BUT WHO'S THE BLAME?
SICKNESS AND DEATH ARE DRIVING ME INSANE.
AS MY BODY IS IN PAIN
I WONDER,
WILL I BE ABLE TO ENDURE THE CHAINS OF STRAIN?
IN A HOLE,
TO WEAK TO GET OUT
NEED PRAYER AND STRENGTH FROM MY SPOUSE.
WHILE MOTHERS ARE CRYING,
AND BROTHERS ARE DYING,
PRAY FOR ME.
THE WORLD IS HARD.
HEARTS ARE SCARRED.
WHILE SATAN SITS BACK,
LAUGHS AND GRINS,
SAYING TO HIMSELF I KNOW   I'M GOING TO WIN. FEAR NOT
THE BATTLE ISN'T YOURS.
FOR SATAN IS ALREADY DEFEATED,
GOD WILL GIVE SATAN THE PAIN THAT'S NEEDED.
SO THERE'S NO REASON TO ACT DEMANDING,
NO REASON TO WHINE,
FOR THE "PEACE THAT PASSES ON UNDERSTANDING, SHALL
GUARD YOUR HEART AND MINE,
THROUGH CHRIST JESUS

# STAY POSITIVE

I'M STILL PRAYING,
UNABLE TO SETTLE
WORKING AT THIS JOB TRYING TO GET A METAL
I'M STILL STRUGGLING!
SHOULD I GO TO WORK TODAY?
I HAVE TO MAINTAIN MY PLACE OF STAY.
DROWNING IN A SEA OF BILLS,
BUT MY EYES STILL LOOK TO THE HILLS.
PEOPLE SIT AROUND WITH NOWHERE TO GO,
AND NOTHING TO EAT
I'M PRAYING TO GOD, THAT THEY
WILL SEE WHAT I SEE.
WHILE THE MAJORITY OF THE THEM,
ARE SPENDING QUALITY TIME IN PLACES THEY DON'T NEED TO
BE.
I HAVE POWER WITHIN
TO KEEP ME FROM SIN
SOCIETY CAN PERSECUTE ME,
STAB ME,
AND BEAT ME WITH A STICK, I'LL STILL PROVIDE FOR MY FAMILY
EVEN WHEN I'M SICK.
SO I'M PROPER WITH MY PREPARATIONS TO PREVENT A POOR
PERFORMANCE,
WHICH WILL MAKE ME A POSITIVE,
PRODUCTIVE,
PERSON
STAYING POSITIVE THROUGH ALL THE TRIALS, WHILE RUNNING
FOR JESUS AT 100 MILES
THANKING THE LORD FOR HIS PRESENCE AND GLORY,
THAT I MAY LIVE TO TELL MY STORY
HOW I MADE IT OVER.

# PRAY FOR US TOO

DADS ARE GREAT
DADS ARE UNIQUE
I'M TIRED OF FAITHLESS LADIES MAKING US WEAK
WE'RE HERE TO LOVE
WE'RE HERE TO GUIDE
WE'RE HERE TO WATCH OVER
WE'RE HERE TO SUPPLY
SO GIVE US A BREAK.
WE'RE ONLY HUMAN,
REGARDLESS OF OUR STATUS, WE'VE ALL BEEN
CHOSEN.
FORGIVE US MOTHERS
FORGIVE US WIVES
FORGIVE US GIRLFRIENDS
BUT JESUS PAID THE PRICE, FOR YOU AND ME,
AND WITH PRAYER AND FAITH
WE WILL BE WHAT YOU NEED.

# SECTION 2

BELIEVE

# STRONG WORDS

RELAX YOUR MIND
AND LET MY WORDS TAKE CONTROL.
AS I POUR OUT MY LOVE FROM YOUR HEAD TO YOUR TOES.
I'M THE ONE THAT'S HERE FOR YOU
I'M THE ONE WHO BRINGS YOU LIFE
I'M THE ONE WHO COMFORTS YOU AT NIGHT,
YES I AM LOVE.
INSPITE OF THE TRIALS THE DEVIL MAY BRING TO YOU.
KNOW MY LOVE IS TRUE,
AND I WILL DIE FOR YOU.
REMEMBER MY WORDS LIKE YOUR BIRTHDAY
I'M LIKE IT, I'LL NEVER GO AWAY
I'LL BE THERE WHEN YOU SLEEP
I'LL BE THERE WHEN YOU DRINK
I'LL BE THERE WHEN YOU WEEP
I'LL EVEN BE THERE WHEN YOU THINK,
FOR I AM YOUR FIRST LOVE

# WHAT KIND OF GOD DO WE SERVE

WHAT KIND OF GOD DO WE SERVE?
THAT HE CAN MAKE SO MANY RACES,
AND SO MANY DIFFERENT FACES
HE CAN MAKE THE SEASONS CHANGE,
FROM WINTER TO SPRING,
WITHOUT DESTROYING A THING
THE GOD WE SERVE SENT HIS SON ON THIS EARTH, FOR
YOU AND ME.
HE WENT TO THE DEVILS KINGDOM AND DROPPED HIM
TO HIS KNEES.
NOW WE CAN OVERCOME WICKED PRINCIPALITY,
IN THIS CORRUPT REALITY.
THAT WILL ELIMINATE US FROM A MULTITUDE OF
FATALITIES.
HE PROTECTS US FROM HURT, HARM, AND DANGER.
SO HANG YOUR BLESSINGS LIKE A HANGER.
GOD IS GREAT,
WORDS CAN'T EXPLAIN HIM,
SO BEFORE YOU DENY HIM,
TRY HIM.

# I AM

I AM THE AIR.
I AM THE COOL BREEZE THAT RECOMENDS
WE COME TOGETHER IN THE STREETS.
I AM THE HUMIDITY THAT SCORCHES
THE PAVEMENT YOU WALK ON.
I AM THE OXYGEN THAT YOU INHAIL,
AND THE CARBON DIOXIDE YOU EXHAIL,
SO, DID I FAIL?
NO,
THE ONES WHO REFUSE TO PICK UP THEIR CROSS, AND
GO THROUGH THE TRIALS THEIR FACED WITH, THEY
FAILED.
BUT IF YOU JUST HANG ON,
I'LL LET YOU SEE MORE,
FOR PRAYER IS THE KEY,
AND FAITH UNLOCKS THE DOOR.

Love and Intimacy

# SOUL TAMPERING

DEAR GOD, THANK YOU FOR MY LIFE.
THANK YOU FOR MY SOUL.
GIVE ME THE WORDS TO ENLIGHTEN ANOTHER'S
CONTROL
MY SOUL IS INTRIGUED FROM THE TALK OF THE
CENTURY,
AS HER SOFT SWEET VOICE EMBRACES
MY FEELINGS
MY MIND DRIFTS TO A LAND UNDAMAGED
I'M UNABLE TO MANAGE,
THE JOY THAT HAS BEEN POURED INTO MY HEART
MY CUP IS OVERFLOWING,
I can't SPILL A SIP,
EVEN IF I HAVE TO GET A SPONGE,
FOR EVERY DRIP
I WILL ABSORB HER SOOTHING EMOTIONS,
AND
SATURATE MY SPIRIT WITH HER SWEET
INTERFERENCE.
MY LADY IS THE FLESH OF MY FLESH
BONE OF MY BONES,
GOD IS MY WITNESS
I'LL DO WHAT IT TAKES TO KEEP HER AT HOME,
OR IN MY DEN
BUT SOMETIMES GOD WILL GIVE MY LIFE A TRIM,
FOR
TRYING TO PUT HER OVER HIM
LORD FORGIVE ME FOR THAT SIN.

# SUNSHINE

Sunshine is on my mind
When I'm with you
You are as pure as water,
And as moist as dew
Sunshine you are as fresh as air on a cool winter breeze on
Christmas Eve.
Sunshine your eyes are like stars that shine in the pale
moonlight that brightens up my night.
In spite of pain and misery that dwells on the land and
makes me whine,
Saying to myself where's my sunshine?
From east to west and north to south,
I
Know without a doubt,
When a relationship is meant to be it is as hard as a rock,
But as sweet as peas
So as the days go by and time flies,
I still say to myself where's my sunshine?

# AT FIRST SIGHT

SHE'S SO SEXY, WAIT,
I THINK MY HEART JUST STOPPED.
HER BEAUTY IS PRICELESS TO ME.
HER LIPS
HER EYES
HER HAIR
HER NOSE
HER SKIN
MY GOD GIRL, LET ME IN.
I REFUSE TO HURT YOU.
I'LL NEVER BREAK YOU.
I REFUSE TO IGNORE YOU.
I'LL ALWAYS ADORE YOU.
NEVER WILL I CAUSE YOU PAIN.
NEVER WILL I BE A DRAIN.
I REFUSE TO BE ANOTHER STRAIN,
ON YOUR HEART
SO WORRY NOT, FOR I'M YOUR FRESH START.

# DREAM

LOVE SWEET LOVE
LOVE IS LIKE A WISH, THEY CAN COME TRUE.
I WISH I COULD FLY WITH YOU BY MY SIDE.
I WISH I COULD SEE YOUR SMILE,
EVERY TIME I CLOSE MY EYES.
I WISH I COULD MAKE MY MUSIC MIX WITH YOURS.
I WISH OUR LOVE COULD BE HARD LIKE A BOARD.
I WISH YOU COULD CALL ME YOURS.
I WISH I COULD BE YOUR LIGHT.
I WISH I COULD MAKE
YOUR LONELY NIGHTS RIGHT
I PROMISE I WON'T FIGHT.
I KNOW MY WORDS ARE HARD TO SEE.
BUT I WAS TAUGHT
"THE TRUTH SHALL SET YOU FREE."
AND IF YOU BELIEVE IN ME,
I PRAY WE'LL GROW LIKE A TREE.

# EYE CANDY

YOUR EYES ARE HYPNOTIZING TO MY SOUL.
THEY SPARKLE MORE THAN WATER,
AND GLEAM MORE THAN GOLD.
I CHERISH THE EYES
FOR THEY ARE THE WAY TO YOUR SOUL
COLOR PLAYS A BIG PART IN YOUR EYES.
THEY CAN BE GREEN, BROWN, OR EVEN BLUE,
FOR WHEN I LOOK INTO YOUR EYES THERE ALWAYS TRUE.
I GET LOVE FROM YOUR EYES
HEAT FROM YOUR EYES
PASSION FROM YOUR EYES
AND MOST OF ALL DREAMS FROM YOUR EYES
I LIKE TO DREAM ABOUT YOUR EYES
WITH NO INTERUPTIONS, AND NO ONE TO STOP ME
FROM CHERISHING THE BEAUTY THAT GOD BLESSED ME TO SEE.

# DRIFT

I DRIFT ON HER WORDS DAY AFTER DAY.
I FLOAT ON HER SCENT MINUTE AFTER MINUTE.
I NEVER DEALT WITH LOVE ON THIS LEVEL BEFORE.
SHE'S LIKE A WELL FED LEECH SUCKING OUT MY SOUL,
DISSOLVING MY MIND WITH SWEET POISON.
 HER SHADOW INTRIGUES MY EVERY MOVE.
I WANT TO SUCK HER SOUL OUT OF HER HEART,
AND FILL IT TEN TIMES OVER
 WITH NON PAINFUL MEMORIES
DRIFT WITH ME MY LOVE,
DRIFT WITH ME,
DRIFT WITH ME

# MIND CARESSING

WALKING ON THE BEACH,
WITH A HAND FULL OF SAND
THINKING ABOUT THAT WOMAN,
YOU KNOW
THE ONE WHO UNDERSTANDS
LOVE IS LIKE A PETAL THAT GROWS,
BUT SEX IS LIKE A WHISPER THAT NOBODY KNOWS.
LET ME LAY GENTLE STROKES ACROSS YOUR FRAME.
WHILE MY CARESSING WORDS
LUBRICATE YOUR BRAIN.
BE CAREFUL, AS MY SELF MADE OIL
MASSAGE YOUR TOES,
BENEATH YOUR NOSE,
ON YOUR BACKSIDE,
AND BETWEEN YOUR THIGHS
MENTAL ERUPTION AND SEDUCTIVE LUSTING
THAT'S WHAT I'M LAYING OUT BEFORE YOU,
NEVER WILL I IGNORE YOU,
NOW BREATH

# WALK WITH ME

CLOSE YOUR EYES WHERE LOGIC AND MYSTERY WON'T
INTERFERE WITH YOUR VISION.
LET YOUR MIND GO TO A UNIVERSE FILLED WITH
PLEASURE,
CAREFREE,
JUDGELESS THOUGHTS
LISTEN, TAKE YOUR EMOTIONS TO A RELM
THAT CAN'T BE CONTROLLED.
SWEETER THAN PICASSO'S ART,
LOVELIER THAN THE VOICES OF MOZART
RIDE MY RHYTHM,
AS MY PASSION FLOWS
DOWN YOUR VOLUPTUOUS ENGRAVINGS
FEEL THE OCEAN AS IT SPLASHES,
AGAINST THE WALLS AND ROCK
LET MY STIMULATING KISSES SURROUND
YOUR BONES WITH SMOOTH LIQUID
SEEPING THROUGH YOUR PORES
DON'T BE AFRAID TO INDULGE IN IT.
JUST ASK FOR IT.

# A FRAGILE HEART

A FRAGILE HEART
SO SIMPLE, IMPERFECT BUT SWEET,
WHO WANTS TO PLEASE THE WORLD JUSTLY?
BUT WHY, IS THIS WORLD MINE?
I DON'T KNOW
I LOVE THIS WORLD,
BUT DOES THIS WORLD LOVE ME?
I WILL KILL FOR THIS WORLD,
BUT WILL THIS WORLD KILL FOR ME?
I WILL DIE FOR THIS WORLD,
BUT WILL THIS WORLD DIE FOR ME?
I'M CONFUSED, BUT I REFUSE TO LOSE.
GOD HELP ME
HELP ME TO SEE, NOT WHAT YOU SEE,
BUT WHAT YOU WANT ME TO SEE.
GIVE ME THE STRENGTH
TO TAKE CARE OF MY WORLD
MAKE MY WORLD A BETTER AND LOVABLE PLACE.
GIVE ME THE SPIRITUAL GLUE TO MEND THE
FRAGILE HEART BACK TOGETHER.

# I'M SORRY

I'M SORRY; I DIDN'T MEAN TO RUSH YOU.
I DIDN'T MEAN TO MAKE YOU LOVE MY WORDS.
I'M NOT TRYING TO BE A NERD.
I'M JUST TRYING TO SPEAK REAL VERBS.
I'M SORRY YOUR WORDS MAKE ME FEEL SUPERB.
I'M SORRY YOUR EYES ARE TRUE.
YES, YOUR LIPS ARE PERFECT TOO.
I'M SORRY YOUR FRAME DRIVES ME INSANE.
I'M SORRY IF I DISTORTED YOUR BRAIN.
I'M SORRY IF YOU'RE NOT FEELING ME.
I'M SORRY IF I TRIED TO MAKE YOU BELIEVE IN ME.
I PRAY I'LL GET IT RIGHT.
I BELIEVE WE CAN MAKE IT NICE.
I WISH YOU DIDN'T MAKE MY HEART BURN.
WHY DOES MY STOMACH TURN?
I'M SORRY YOU INSPIRE ME.
I WISH YOU WOULD ADMIRE ME.
WHY DO I FEEL LIKE A BOY WHEN I SEE YOU?
WHEN WILL YOU MAKE MY DREAMS COME TRUE?
I'M AS FREE AS A DOVE.
I'M SORRY; I THINK I'M IN LOVE.

# Section 4

Strength too all

# ANSWER ME

ANOTHER DAY I CAN'T SLEEP.
THE DREAM IS TRYING TO EAT AT ME,
PAIN FROM MYSTERY AND UNBELIEF
WHY WON'T SHE BELIEVE ME?
WHY DOES SHE MISLEAD ME?
WHY AT NIGHT, SHE LOVES ME, BUT IN LIGHT
SHE HATES ME?
WHY DO I ALWAYS HAVE SOMETHING TO WRITE ABOUT,
BUT NOTHING TO SAY
WHY, IS MY HEART BROKE?
WHY IS MY HOPE STARTING TO FLOAT?
WHY CAN'T SHE LOVE ME FOR ME?
WHY WON'T SHE EVER BELIEVE ME?
(JESUS PLEASE MAKE IT STOP)
WHY IS THE DEVIL TRYING TO MAKE HER LEAVE?
WHY IS THE DEVIL TRYING TO MAKE ME BLEED?
WHY IS THE DEVIL TRYING TO MAKE US DISAGREE?
WHY DOES SHE THINK SHE'S THE ONLY ONE
IN PAIN
WHY DOES SHE HATE ON MY FRAME?
WHY DOES SHE FEEL LIKE SHE'S THE ONLY ONE THAT CAN
CHANGE?
WHY CAN'T SHE TALK TO ME?
WHY DOES SHE TREAT ME LIKE I'M THE
ONE WHO TOOK IT, "G"?
CAN YOU FEEL ME!
WHY DOESN'T SHE TRUST HER MAN?
WHY DOESN'T SHE CALL HER MAN A MAN?
WHY CAN'T SHE LET HIM BE A MAN?
WHY DOES SHE THINK I'M A JOKE?
WHY DOESN'T SHE BELIEVE I LOVE HER LIKE A YOKE,
THAT CAN'T BE BROKE?
HOW COME I'M TALKING, BUT NO ONE CAN HEAR ME.
WILL SOME ONE PLEASE ANSWER ME?

Strength too all

# LADIES

LADIES COME IN ALL SHAPES, SIZES, COLOR,
AND FASHIONS.
THEY CAN BE SWIFT AS A FOX WITH THE
SWEETEST OF PASSION.
IT DOESN'T MATTER IF THEIR YELLOW, BLACK,
OR WHITE,
THEY'RE ALL MEEK IN GODS SIGHT.
SOME CAN BE SMOOTH AS A SNAKE,
ON A COOL SANDY PATH.
SO FOR THE MAN THAT LIKES TO PLAY GAMES
YOU BETTER WATCH YOUR BACK.
A MEAN LADY CAN BITE HARD LIKE A PIT BULL
THEN ACT CONTENT AS A DOVE
BUT SWEET AS THEY ARE,
YOU KNOW THERE FROM ABOVE.
SO MEN WHEN YOU FIND A LADY THAT FITS LIKE
A GLOVE,
YOU KNOW IT HAS TO BE LOVE.
TO THE LADIES THAT'S DIRTY AND PHONY,
BEWARE, BECAUSE IN THE END YOU'LL ALWAYS
BE BROKE AND LONELY.
TO CONCLUDE MY WORDS,
LADIES DON'T BE CONCEITED AND DEMANDING,
FOR GOD WILL SEND YOU A MAN WITH LOVE AND
UNDERSTANDING.

# BROTHERS

BROTHERS WE WANT
BROTHERS WE NEED
WHEN ONE FALLS DOWN, ANOTHERS ON HIS KNEES,
PRAYING TO SEE
IF WE'LL SUCCEED IN OUR FIERY TRIALS ON THE
STREETS
DESTROY ONE SEED
YOU INCREASE THE PAIN THAT MAKES A BROTHER
SAY MAN,
I CAN'T STAND IT.
O GOD, SEND THE RAIN,
SEND THE SNOW,
JUST GET ME OUT OF THIS HELL HOLE.
BROTHERS, WE ARE STRONG WHEN WE CAN GET
ALONG.
SO TAKE HEED TO THE SPIRITUAL LYRICS I
SPEEK.
PROCEED TO DISSOLVE,
AND INVOLVE YOUR SELF IN THIS SPIRITUAL WAR
TO OPEN MORE DOORS FOR OUR BROTHERS

# CLARITY

WHAT IS CLARITY?
CLARITY IS CLEAR.
KNOW HOW CAN IT,
WHAT EVER IT IS, BE CLEAR TO YOU
IF YOUR MIND IS CLOUDY WITH MILDEW
SPENDING TIME WITH YOUR MIND OUT OF YOUR
BODY, AND YOUR BODY OUT OF YOUR MIND
CONFUSING THOUGHTS WITH UNPARALLEL
WALKS WILL SEND YOUR SPIRIT TO A MULTITUDE
OF DIVISION. WHICH MAKES YOUR SOUL SPLIT
INTO SEPARATE DEMINSION
FOR SOMEONE TO TRULY UNDERSTAND WHAT
CLEAR IS, THEY MUST IGNORE THE VOICES THEY
HEAR, AND TAKE A LONG LOOK IN THE MIRROR.

## TIRED

TIRED OF UPS
TIRED OF DOWN
TIRED OF GOING AROUND LIKE A MERRY GO ROUND
WHEN IT STOPS NOBODY KNOWS,
THE TROUBLE THAT SEEKS ME
(STOP JESUS HELP ME)
SO TIRED OF THE NEGITIVE UNTRUST LIKE STORIES
THAT'S MAKING YOU WORRY.
I NEED YOU TO SEE ME,
NOT WHAT YOU THINK YOU SEE.
I NEED YOU TO FEEL ME,
NOT WHAT YOU THINK YOU FEEL.
DON'T ALLOW SATAN TO STEAL,
KILL
AND DESTROY WHAT WE BUILD.
BEFORE OUR LOVE START TO PEEL
SO LOVE CHILL.

Strength too all
# UNSUCCESSFUL THIEF
## (VOICES IN MY HEAD)


WHO DO YOU THINK YOU ARE?
YOU'RE A NOBODY
YOU CAN'T WIN
WHY DO YOU PRAY?
NO ONE IS LISTENING TO YOU.
(JUST STOP)
WHY DON'T YOU GIVE UP?
YOU DON'T DESERVE THAT NICE CAR.
YOUR LIFE IS LIKE A CLOSED JAR, IT'S CONCEALED.
YOU HAVE NO WILL
(JUST STOP)
WHAT ARE YOU DOING IN MY WORLD?
WHAT ARE YOU DOING WITH THAT PRETTY GIRL?
WHY ARE YOU HERE?
WHY DON'T YOU JUMP OFF A PIER?
NOBODY CARES
YOU'RE NOT GOING TO MAKE IT
I'M GOING TO TAKE IT.
I'M GOING TO KILL YOU,
(KILL ME, YOU COULDN'T KILL ME WHEN YOU HAD ME.)
(HOW ARE YOU GOING TO KILL ME NOW)
(JUST STOP, STOP, STOP I SAY.)
(GOD HAS MY BACK, AND I'LL RIDE THAT WAVE.)
(YOU SEE, YOU CAN'T STOP ME, JESUS IS WITH ME.)
(TO THE TOP IS WHERE I'LL BE)
(KNOW TAKE THAT THIEF)

# SECTION 5

*God is a protector*

## COVERED

QUIET, I THINK SOMEONE'S OUT THERE.
FEELING THE PURE INTENSITY OF FEAR,
AS IT FLOWS THROUGH MY BLOOD
THE CREEPY NOISE INHANCES MY HEART BEAT;
IT'S BEATING SO HARD YOU CAN HEAR IT BEATING
DOWN THE STREET.
WHAT SHOULD I DO?
NOWHERE TO RUN,
NOWHERE TO HIDE
PRAYING, SAYING TO MYSELF,
I DON'T WANT TO DIE.
FIGHTING A WAR SOMEONE ELSE STARTED.
TELLING MYSELF IT'S TIME FOR US TO DEPART,
FROM THIS CORRUPT CITY.
FIGHITING AGAIST PEOPLE WHO HAVE NO PITTY
SHHH, THE PHONE RINGS
I WAS SO SPOOKED I JUMPED LIKE A SPRING.
HAND ON THE TRIGGER,
SO FULL OF FRIGHT,
SAYING TO MYSELF SOMEONE DYING TONIGHT
THEN THE VOICE OF THE LORD SAID TO ME FEAR
NOT,
FOR I'M WITH THEE,
AND ONCE I FELT A CHILL,
I KNEW GOD WAS WITH ME.

*God is a protector*

# PEACE OF MIND

AS THE SAND SETTLES,
AND THE SUN SETS.
I'M ALONE AGAIN WITH MY BOY CHECK,
CHECK AND I HAD SOME TIMES,
WE DID.
FROM SHOOTING AT PROBLEMS,
AND SPLITING ENEMY WIGS.
I TAKE ADVANTAGE OF THE
QUIET STILL NIGHTS
IT ALLOWS ME TO CLEAN CHECK,
NICE AND TIGHT.
I EVEN READ STORY TO HIM
AND KISS HIM GOOD NIGHT.
I WAKE UP FROM MY REST,
PRAYING
THANKING GOD FOR THE FRESH AIR.
WAR IS HARD,
BUT I WILL MAKE IT
NOT WORRING ABOUT MY PROBLEMS,
LET GOD TAKE CARE OF IT.
SO I'LL LACE MY BOOTS UP TIGHT,
AND MAKE SURE CHECK IS RIGHT.
THANKING GOD FOR TODAY,
AND NOT WORRY ABOUT TONIGHT.

*God is a protector*

# SILENT NIGHT

NIGHT COMES UPON ME.
PARANOIA TRIES TO DESTROY ME.
AS THE DARK LORD WHISPERS
EVIL NOTHINGS IN MY EAR
DRIVING ME TO A PIER, NOT TO JUMP, BUT TO
DUMP
ON WHO EVER TRIES TO HURT ME OR MY FAMILY
BUT IT'S NOT ABOUT ME
IT'S ABOUT WHO WANT'S TO MEET WHAT LIES
BENEATH.
BENEATH THE DIRT
BENEATH THE HURT
BENEATH THE CRAFTY SPIRIT THAT LURKS
IN THE DARK WITHOUT A SPARK OF JOY
SEEKING WHO HE MAY DESTROY
SO PREPARE YOURSELF FOR THE SILENT NIGHT
FOR YOU KNOW NOT WHEN YOU'LL HAVE TO FIGHT.

*God is a protector*

# RUNNING OUT OF TIME

PEOPLE, CAN YOU HEAR IT
THE CRY OF WEAK EMPTY SOULS
CRAVING FOR SPIRITUAL GUIDANCE,
TO ENHANCE THEIR THOUGHT PATTERNS ON LIFE
AND DEATH.
WHAT IS THE MEANING OF LIFE?
WHAT IS THE PURPOSE OF DEATH?
WHERE WILL YOU GO WHEN YOU RUN OUT OF
BREATH?
TIME WAITS FOR KNOW MAN
WE ALL NEED TO KNOW THAT.
LOVE GOD
BELIEVE IN GOD
HAVE FAITH IN GOD
DON'T WAIT TO LATE FOR GOD.

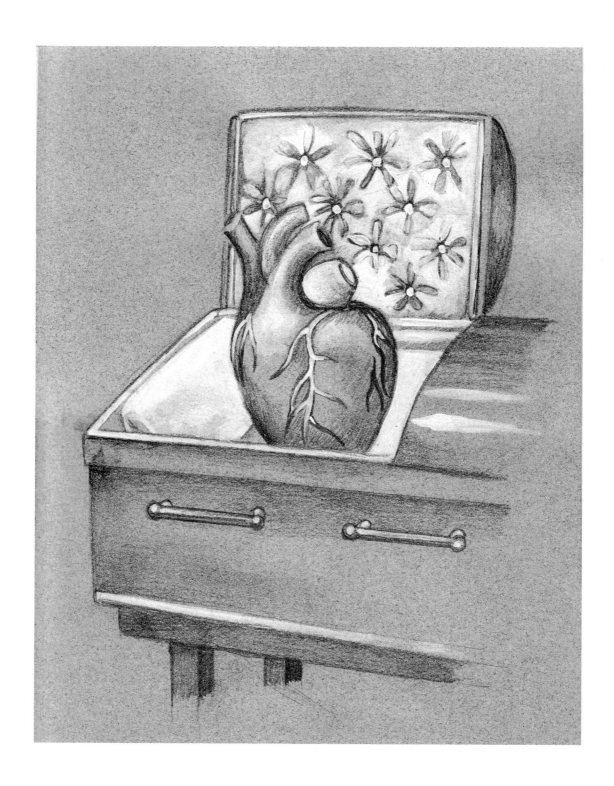

## DEATH THROUGH THE WIND

SMOKE THIS,
NO, I DON'T WANT TO SMOKE ANYMORE.
WHY?
I DON'T WANT TO GET HIGH.
WHAT ABOUT SOME COCAIN,
NOW THAT'S JUST NOT SANE.
RIDING IN A WHITE CADILLAC,
WITH MY BROTHER BY MY SIDE
ALL RIGHT THEN, BUT I DON'T WANT TO DIE.
POW, POW, THE DRAMA BEGINS
I FEEL DEATH COMING THROUGH THE WIND.
RIDING IN PEORIA, THAT'S ANOTHER STORY.
THOSE BOYS ON SMITH STREET, YEA
THEY KNEW HOW TO PUT IT DOWN,
WHEN TIMES GOT ROUGH WE HAD TO CLOWN.
POW, POW, THE DRAMA BEGINS
I FEEL DEATH COMING THROUGH THE WIND.
BLACK SMOKE AND FLAMES
BLAZING AT MY BRAIN
WHILE MY BOY HAD TO JUMP THROUGH A WINDOW
FRAME.
I ROLLED ON THE FLOOR,
I CAN'T TAKE ANYMORE
SWEAT, HEAT, FULL OF FEAR
I KNOW DEATH IS NEAR.
OUT THE HOUSE TO A SAFE PLACE TO SET UP,
SAYING TO MYSELF JESUS, JESUS, JESUS, JESUS,
JESUS

# JESUS, JESUS

## *God is a protector*

### BOTTOM LINE

THE BOTTOM, YEA THAT'S A START.
100 GD'S STANDING IN THE PARK.
ALL LOVE, NO FLAWS,
EVERONE THERE LEARING ABOUT THE LAW
MEN AMONGST MEN, NO BOYS, BUT REAL TOYS
ADJUSTING TO THE ENVIRONMENT
NO, I'M NOT GLORIFING IT,
JUST NOT DENYING IT.
LET'S NOT FORGET ABOUT THOSE BD'S,
AND UNDERCOVER COPS TRYING TO ORDER MARTINIS
PEORIA IS A BIG TRAP
THE JOBS ARE LIKE A DROUGHT
PRAYING TO GOD MY BOYS MAKE IT OUT.
DRAMA IS A WAY OF LIFE IN THE P.
FILLED WITH VICE LORDS, BD'S AND GD'S.
SO YOU'RE CHOICE BETTER SMART.
THERE ARE A LOT OF WEAK ONES,
THAT WILL GET YOU CAUGHT UP IN THE DARK.
BUT GODS LOVE WILL GIVE YOU THAT SPARK,
SO YOU CAN SEE, AND NOT BE BOUND, BUT FREE.
GD

# SECTION 6

Mental Thoughts

# THEY

HOW CAN THEY, WHOEVER THEY ARE, HATE ME?
THEY DON'T EVEN KNOW ME.
THEY TRY TO DESTROY ME.
THEY ALWAYS IGNORE ME.
THEY CAN BE BLACK.
THEY CAN BE WHITE.
THEY DON'T KNOW MY FIGHT.
THEY WILL WATCH ME IN MY BENZ.
THEY CAN BE FAMILY FROM WITHIN.
THEY CLAIM THEY LOVE YOU.
THEY SAY MY WORDS ARE TRUE.
THEY ACT LIKE THEY SUPPORT YOU.
THEY REALLY DON'T KNOW WHAT IT TOOK.
THEY WANT EVEN BUY MY BOOK.
THEY DON'T WANT MY KIDS TO EAT.
THEY DON'T WANT ME TO LIVE LIKE A KING.
THEY DON'T WANT ME TO DRIVE SOMETHING MEAN.
JESUS, WHY DON'T THEY JUST LEAVE?

## Mental Thoughts

A bad situation is only
A blessing in progress

------------------------------------

Having faith is the first
Step to becoming a man

– – – – – – – – – – – – – –

Life is to short
Don't waste it complaining

/////////////////////////////

Don't put love and lust
Together, for love will grow
And lust will just go away

– – – – – – – – – – – – – – –

People listen to what they
Want to hear, and don't hear
What they need to listen to

-------------------------------------------

I'M lost because you're
Lost will you lead me

/////////////////////////////

Think before every decision,
Because it might be your last

– – – – – – – – – – – – –

NEVER BELIEVE IN BELIEVING, UNLESS YOU
KNOW WHAT YOU ARE BELIEVING IN IS
WORTH BELIEVING

TRYING TO DO IT
WITHOUT TRYING HARD AT IT
WILL JUST LEAVE YOU TRYING TO SEE IT

HOW CAN YOU GUARANTEE, THAT YOURSELF
WOULD BE ALRIGHT,
IF YOU DO NOT KNOW YOURSELF
LEAVING YOURSELF IN A STATE,
WITHOUT YOURSELF
 KNOW WHO YOU ARE FIRST

LOVE IS THE GREATEST POWER
KNOWN TO MAN, SO DON'T ABUSE IT

THANK YOU GOD FOR THE SPIRIT TO
LISTEN AND THE WILL TO WRITE


SPECIAL THANKS TO MY FAMILY AND FRIENDS,
I LOVE YOU AND THANK YOU FOR YOUR SUPPORT.


SPECIAL THANKS TO THE 1st SEMI PRO
FOOTBALL TEAM IN ARKANSAS,
(THE ARKANSAS RHINOS)
SOME OF THE MOST TALENTED PLAYERS
YOU'LL EVER SEE.
(STAY HEALTHY COMRADES)


P.S. GOD PROTECT AND WATCH OVER MY COMRADES IN
PEORIA
ILLINOIS, LOVE AND STAY UP.

Be on the look out for volume 2
RESURRECTED DEMONS
COMPRESSED AND DEFEATED


THANK YOU FOR GIVING ME A FEW MINUTES OF YOUR
TIME. I HOPE MY EXPERIENCES, FEELINGS, AND TRIALS IN LIFE

WERE ABLE TO ENLIGHTEN, TEACH, OR EVEN PREPARE YOU FOR SITUATIONS YOU MAY HAVE TO FACE. ONE OF THE MAIN TOOLS IN LIFE IS TO HAVE FAITH IN GOD, AND IN YOUR SELF. AN AUTHOR BY THE NAME OF *LEO TOLSTOY* WROTE A SHORT STORY ENTITLED, "*THE DEATH OF IVAN ILLYCH.*" IT WAS ABOUT A MAN WHO BELIEVED HIS LIFE WAS A LIE. HE BELIEVED HE SPENT HIS TIME BEING WHAT EVERYONE ELSE WANTED HIM TO BE AND NOT WHAT HE WANTED TO BE. I BELIEVE, WE AS PEOPLE HAVE THAT SAME PROBLEM. WE'RE ALWAYS TRYING TO BE LIKE SOMEONE ELSE, LOOK LIKE SOMEONE ELSE, OR EVEN SMELL LIKE SOMEONE ELSE.

WHEN WE SHOULD TRY TO BE LIKE THE ONE WHO DIED FOR OUR SINS! I LOVE ALL RACES, AND CHERISH THE DIFFERENCES IN ALL OF THEM. BELIEVING IN GOD AND BEING TAUGHT ABOUT GOD WAS THE BEST THING THAT EVER HAPPENED TO ME. I LOVE GOD, MY FAMILY, AND PRAY WHO EVER READS THIS BOOK, WILL BE BLESSED 100 FOLD.

Printed in Great Britain
by Amazon

80390056R00041